D1583157

Dreadful Droughts

TURRIFF ACADEMY
LIBRARY
★

Heinemann
LIBRARY

Louise and Richard Spilsbury

www.heinemann.co.uk/library
Visit our website to find out more information about **Heinemann Library** books.

To order:
 Phone 44 (0) 1865 888066
 Send a fax to 44 (0) 1865 314091
Visit the Heinemann Bookshop at www.heinemann.co.uk/library to browse our catalogue and order online.

First published in Great Britain by Heinemann Library, Halley Court, Jordan Hill, Oxford OX2 8EJ, part of Harcourt Education.
Heinemann is a registered trademark of Harcourt Education Ltd.

© Harcourt Education Ltd 2003
The moral right of the proprietor has been asserted.

All rights reserved. No part of this publication may be reproduced, stored in a retrieval system, or transmitted in any form or by any means, electronic, mechanical, photocopying, recording, or otherwise, without either the prior written permission of the publishers or a licence permitting restricted copying in the United Kingdom issued by the Copyright Licensing Agency Ltd, 90 Tottenham Court Road, London W1T 4LP (www.cla.co.uk).

Editorial: Andrew Farrow and Dan Nunn
Design: David Poole and Paul Myerscough
Illustrations: Geoff Ward
Picture Research: Rebecca Sodergren and Debra Weatherley
Production: Edward Moore

Originated by Dot Gradations Limited
Printed in Hong Kong, China by Wing King Tong

ISBN 0 431 17829 1
07 06 05 04 03
10 9 8 7 6 5 4 3 2 1

British Library Cataloguing in Publication Data
Spilsbury, Richard, 1963 –
Dreadful droughts. – (Awesome Forces of Nature)
1. Droughts – Juvenile literature
I. Title II. Spilsbury, Louise
551.5′773
A full catalogue record for this book is available from the British Library.

Acknowledgements
The publishers would like to thank the following for permission to reproduce photographs:

Associated Press pp. **10**, **28**; Corbis pp. **6** (Galen Rowell), **15** (Paul A. Souders); Das Fotoarchive pp. **12**, **13**, **22**; Getty News and Sport p. **21**; Magnum p. **27** (C. Steele Perkins); Panos Pictures p. **18** (Clive Shirley); Rex Features pp. **5**, **11**, **17**, **19** (SIPA Press); Science Photo Library p. **23**; Still Pictures p. **16**; Trip pp. **4** (B. Gibbs), **8** (Dinodia), **25** (Eric Smith).

Cover photograph reproduced with permission of Corbis.

Every effort has been made to contact copyright holders of any material reproduced in this book. Any omissions will be rectified in subsequent printings if notice is given to the publishers.

TURRIFF ACADEMY LIBRARY

Contents

Any words appearing in the text in bold, **like this**, are explained in the Glossary.

What is a drought?

A drought happens when an area that usually gets rain has too little water for a long time. It badly affects the lives and health of the plants, people and other animals living there. All living things depend on water in some way – our bodies are mostly made up of water and we cannot live without water for longer than a few days.

Plants need water to grow properly and animals need water to drink. We use water to cook our food, to keep clean and to carry away our waste. Water is used to make electricity for homes, factories and power plants. Factories also use water to cool and clean machinery. When there is a shortage of water, all of these things are affected.

Not all droughts are deadly. A minor drought during the summer in the UK may simply mean that people have to water their lawns and crops. They can use stored or tap water while they wait for rain to come.

Devastating droughts

A major drought is one that affects a large area and a great many living things for a very long time. Droughts in parts of Africa can last for years. Without enough water, farmers may not be able to grow **crops** for several years in a row. People and their farm animals have so little food to eat that they become ill and may die.

DROUGHT FACTS

❗ From space Earth looks like a blue planet because 80 per cent of its surface is covered in water.

❗ Most water on Earth is salt water. Only 2 per cent is fresh water that we can drink.

❗ One of the world's biggest problems is providing clean, fresh water for everyone.

Drought is serious in poorer countries, such as Somalia in Africa. Poor people do not have enough money to buy food and water and their government may not be able to help them.

What causes droughts?

Droughts happen when not enough rain falls on an area of land. It may still rain once in a while. However, the rain that falls dries up quickly afterwards and does not really help.

What causes rain?

When water at the surface of the world's oceans and rivers warms up, it evaporates. This means that the warm air turns it from liquid water into a gas in the air that we cannot see, called water **vapour**. When a patch of air gets pushed high into the air the water vapour in it cools down again. The water vapour turns back into droplets of water. They are so small and light that they float in the air and cling to tiny bits of dust in the air. Clumps of the droplets gather together to form clouds that we can see. Eventually the water droplets become so large and heavy that they fall from the clouds as rain.

A cloud is a large clump of very tiny droplets of water.

Why does it stop raining?

Water vapour only turns back into droplets of water if the air it is in rises into the colder parts of the sky. If the air does not rise, then no clouds form. Without clouds, there is no rain.

Air rises and falls depending on **air pressure**. Most people have heard weather **forecasters** talk about high and low-**pressure systems**. It is quite a complicated subject, but basically the difference is that when there is high air pressure, air does not rise. Air only rises when there is low air pressure.

What is air pressure?

Sometimes the air above Earth is pushed together. Scientists call this a high-pressure system. This brings clear, dry weather. Sometimes the air is not quite so pushed together. This is a low-pressure system. It brings cloudy, rainy weather.

The lines on this weather map show pressure systems over Europe. High-pressure systems are marked 'H' and low-pressure systems are marked 'L'. These systems are constantly moving and changing. Weather is usually wet in low-pressure areas, and dry in high-pressure areas.

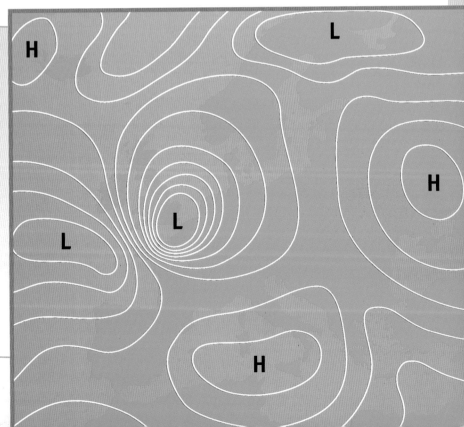

Pressure systems

High-pressure systems and low-pressure systems usually move around all the time. That is why most countries get some rainy days and some dry days. Sometimes high-pressure systems stay over the same place for a long time. They may be held in place by wide, fast-moving air **currents** high in the sky.

Sometimes, cold or warm water currents in the oceans can change the way the wind moves. This can also stop pressure systems from moving on. For example, a giant warm current called **El Niño** can keep high-pressure systems over countries in Asia, such as India. When a high-pressure system stays too long, it can cause drought.

In parts of Asia, summer winds usually blow rain clouds like these north from the Indian Ocean. As the clouds pass over land they bring the monsoon season. This is when it rains almost every day for weeks on end. If the rain clouds do not come, there is drought.

Where do droughts happen?

Droughts can happen in nearly any area of land in the world. They happen most often in places with hot and dry **climates**, such as parts of Africa, the USA, Australia and India. Droughts happen less often in places with wetter climates, such as Scandinavia and the north and south **poles**.

Droughts cause most problems in places where people need lots of water to grow **crops** or for their **livestock** to drink. In some of these places, such as southern parts of the USA, droughts ruin massive areas of crops. This is bad for farmers because it means they make less money than usual. In other places, such as Somalia in Africa, droughts can result in people starving. When their food plants and animals die, poor people have nothing to eat. They may die unless they are given help.

The red patches on this map show the areas on Earth which receive the least rain. When droughts happen, they affect drier areas worse than wetter areas.

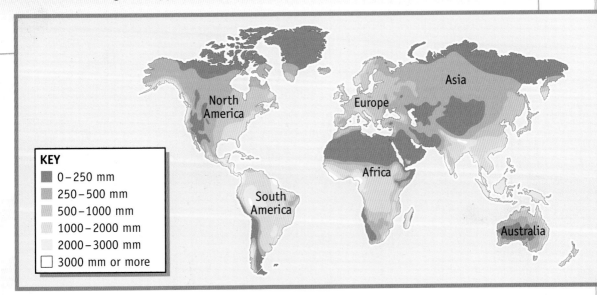

KEY
- 0 – 250 mm
- 250 – 500 mm
- 500 – 1000 mm
- 1000 – 2000 mm
- 2000 – 3000 mm
- 3000 mm or more

North America
South America
Europe
Asia
Africa
Australia

What happens in a drought?

The first signs of drought are when grass turns brown and other plants **wilt**. As **groundwater** dries up, cracks appear across the land.

After a few weeks, plants start to die. When plant roots shrivel they no longer bind the soil together. The soil is then **eroded** by wind. Sometimes enough dust gets blown into the air to form giant dust storms. Bare patches of soil get hotter than those covered in plants. In some places **wildfires** may start. These will spread quickly through any remaining dry plants.

Affecting future crops

Topsoil is the top layer of soil on the ground. It is more fertile (good for growing **crops**) than the soil below. If wind and rain erode topsoil, the soil that is left is less fertile. This means that future crops cannot grow so well.

Some droughts can go on for over five or even ten years.

Animals in a drought

During a drought, animals cannot find enough to drink or to eat. They may also suffer from heat stroke – an illness caused by getting too hot. As plants die, plant-eating animals such as wildebeest or sheep have to travel further to find food. As they move, they erode the dry soil with their hooves. Many die of hunger and **dehydration**. Then carnivores – animals that eat other animals – such as lions cannot catch enough prey and they begin to starve.

Some animals benefit from the death of other animals. **Scavengers** such as hyenas or vultures eat dead animals. But the bodies of dead animals are also places where **bacteria** grow. When flies feed on the bodies they pick up bacteria and spread diseases to other animals.

In times of drought, all animals are at risk of dying of dehydration – when there is not enough water for their bodies to work properly.

Lakes, reservoirs and rivers

During a drought, the water levels in lakes, **reservoirs** and rivers are lower. Animals that live there have fewer places to breed (have babies) or shelter. When rivers or streams stop flowing into lakes and reservoirs, the water becomes **stagnant**. Fish and other animals that breathe oxygen in water then suffocate (die from lack of oxygen).

Using less water

People in villages, towns and cities have to use less water in a drought. They must have enough water to drink. They have to cut down on how much water they use for cooking and how often they wash or flush toilets. Factories and **power plants** also have to reduce the amount they use.

Some plants, called algae, thrive in stagnant water. They can take over lakes and reservoirs. They may also produce poisons that kill animals and other plants that share the water.

Famine

A **famine** is when a large number of people do not have enough to eat. It is often the result of a serious drought. When drought kills crops and plants that **livestock** usually eat, many poor people go hungry. If people do not have enough food they become weak and may die from **malnutrition**. If there is not enough clean water, they may have to drink any dirty water they can find. This means they may catch diseases that cause **diarrhoea** and dehydration.

DROUGHT FACTS

! In nearly every part of the world farmers are more likely to be affected by drought than by any other natural disaster.

! Drought has killed more people than any other natural disaster.

! Across the world, drought has been responsible for millions of deaths and hundreds of billions of dollars in damage in the last 50 years.

If their livestock dies, people affected by drought may have nothing to sell in order to buy food.

Eastern Australia, 1994

Australia is one of the driest continents on Earth. Because of this, drought is a part of Australia's **climate** and the government does not usually consider it to be a natural disaster, except in extraordinary circumstances like those in 1994. In that year, conditions in eastern Australia were among the driest since records began. A large part of the country officially had its worst drought of the twentieth century.

The cause of the drought was warm **El Niño** sea **currents** off South America that changed the movement of winds across a large area. This meant rain clouds were not blown over eastern Australia from the Pacific Ocean. Some rain did fall, but not anything like as much as usual. **Reservoirs** and rivers dried up and water had to be delivered to many towns in the countryside for up to a year.

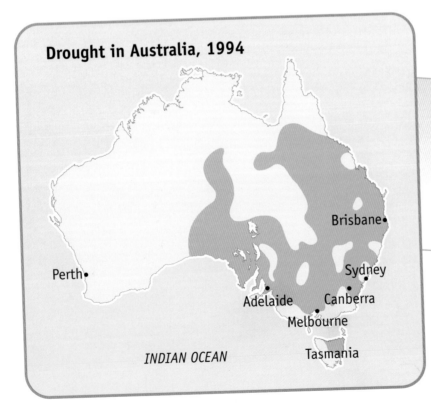

Drought in Australia, 1994

Perth•

Brisbane•

Sydney•

Adelaide•   Canberra•

Melbourne•

INDIAN OCEAN   Tasmania

This map shows the areas of Eastern Australia that were most affected by the drought of 1994.

Drought damages

The drought damaged many wild plants and killed large areas of **crops** and **pasture**. Then the price of animal foods, such as grain, went up. This meant that farmers could not afford to keep much **livestock**. Life for farmers became impossible – they had fewer cattle and sheep to sell and had more food to buy. Many farmers were forced to give up. They went to live and work in big towns.

'The worst thing is we have lost neighbours on both sides. They were not only neighbours but were our friends.' **A Queensland farmer**

Moving wildlife

When there are fewer plants to eat, wild animals come into towns looking for food. Thousands of wild mice ruined large areas of crops worth millions of dollars as they travelled across farmland.

At one point, 30 families a week were leaving their farms for good because they could not afford to live there any more.

Who helps when droughts happen?

A drought is a natural event like an **earthquake**. The difference between a drought and most other natural events is that a drought builds up very slowly. People need more help as a drought lasts longer.

Rich and poor

Droughts affect wealthy countries less than poor countries because:

- they can afford to store larger amounts of food and water
- they have more pipes and canals, and more vehicles to transport water when it runs out
- they can buy food if their supplies run out or if **crops** fail
- people have more radios and TVs to receive drought warnings
- they can afford larger **emergency services** and armed forces with better equipment to help when a drought hits
- richer governments can afford to help farmers affected by drought.

Poor people may rely on wells for their water and have few other places to get clean water.

Rationing

When water and food are in short supply, people must take care it does not run out. Government workers do this by rationing, which means controlling the amount that each person can use. At first rations are quite generous. If a drought goes on for a long time they become smaller. For example, rationing at the beginning of a drought may mean people can use water normally except that they cannot water their lawns. Later on, rations may only be enough for essential uses – drinking, cooking and some washing. When stored water runs out, it has to be brought in from elsewhere.

Extreme rationing

In some countries, police fine or even imprison people who use more than their share of water or steal food. In severe droughts, the army or police sometimes guard wells and stores of food.

In the 1989 drought in the UK, some people had to get their water from tanks left in the street.

On the move

Poor people often have to move away from places that are badly affected by drought. They travel to areas where they will find food and water. They are known as **refugees**. When lots of refugees gather in one place, they use up the stored food and water there. Many refugees are too weak to travel any further.

Local emergency services and **volunteers** give out rations of food and water. They may also provide some medical care and shelter for the refugees. Usually they also need help from other countries.

Emergencies

The police, fire and ambulance services and the army have to help out when drought causes other problems. For example, **firefighters** have to put out forest fires that burn dry trees. Medical workers treat people for the effects of smoke and heat from the fires.

Refugees usually take as many of their possessions as they can with them when they move to escape a threat such as drought.

Types of aid

The help that people give to those in need is called **aid**. Money, food, medicines, blankets and clothes are all kinds of aid. Governments and large organizations in other countries often send aid to countries in need. People like you also give aid by sending donations (gifts of money) to local, national or international **charities**. After a big drought, charities such as the Red Cross or Oxfam have special appeals asking for donations so they can help people in need quickly.

There are different kinds of aid. For example, charities may provide new lorries to transport water or food to people who need it. Or they may send tools and materials so people can dig better wells for themselves. They may also send equipment to build larger **reservoirs** to store more water for future droughts.

*In times of drought, trained medical workers can help to treat **malnutrition** or **dehydration**.*

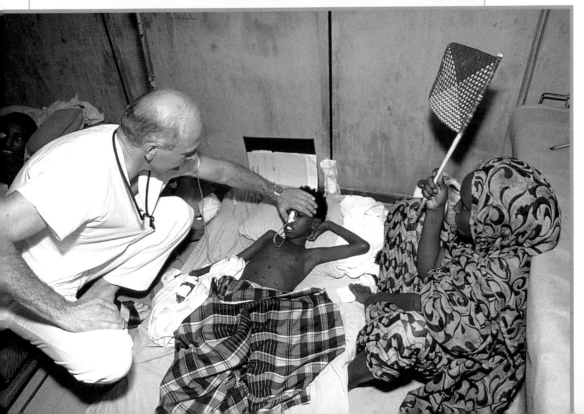

USA, 1998 to 2002

From 1998 to 2002, far less rain and snow than usual fell over large areas of eastern and midwestern USA. In some parts, a whole year's worth of rain did not arrive, so rivers, lakes and **reservoirs** dried up. By summer 2002, around one-third of the USA was experiencing a severe drought.

Plants were extremely dry, winds were strong and temperatures were high. These were ideal conditions for **wildfires**. There were at least twice as many wildfires as usual. Several states coped with the fires by giving jobs to extra **firefighters** and buying extra fire-fighting equipment such as aircraft that drop water.

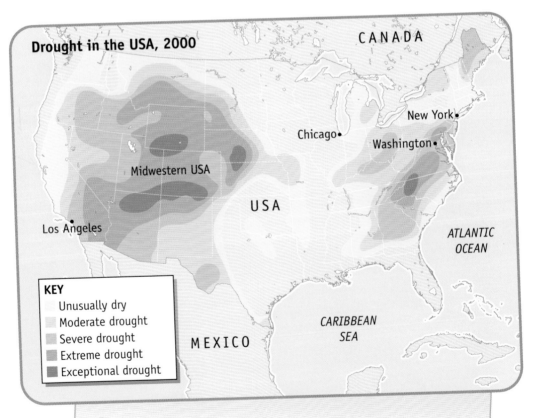

In summer 2000, many parts of the USA suffered extreme drought conditions. The worst affected areas are shown in red. The drought lasted until 2002.

Saving water

In the US state of Maine, half the people in the countryside get their water from shallow wells. Many of these dried up during the drought. Most people could not afford to dig deeper wells to reach deeper **groundwater**. Many had to drive trucks into towns to fill containers of water. They had to conserve (save) water in any way they could.

'We started using paper plates to eat off and using our pasta water to flush the toilet. I even rinsed my hair in the dog's drinking bucket.'
Cynthia Novacek, Maine

Saving water in towns and cities was just as important. New York usually uses one billion gallons of water a year. In the drought, businesses were supplied with less water. People were ordered not to use water to wash pavements or cars, or water lawns, especially during hotter parts of the day.

During the drought, New York public fountains like this one were shut down to remind people about the need to conserve water.

Can droughts be predicted?

The cost of dealing with the effects of drought can be great. Therefore many people try to predict when they may strike, so that preparations can be made in advance. People make predictions by studying **climate** and weather patterns.

Past climate

Have you ever seen the growth rings on cut-down trees or logs? Similar rings can be seen in **coral**. One of the ways scientists know about climate in the past is by looking at these rings! Both trees and coral grow more in wet years, producing wider rings. They grow less in dry years, which means the rings are narrower.

Growth rings suggest that droughts happen in cycles (repeated patterns). In Australia they happen on average every eighteen years. If people know how long the drought cycle in a country is, they can predict when a drought is likely to happen next.

By looking at the pattern of growth rings in trees, scientists can work out when there were extremely dry years in the past.

Weather

Scientists predict droughts by working out how the weather will affect the land. They measure and record how hot it is, and how much rain or snow falls. They also measure how high the water is in rivers and **reservoirs**, and how dry the soil is. They use **satellites** in space and aircraft to take photos of rainclouds all over the Earth. By measuring the speed and directions of the wind and the **air pressure**, they work out how fast and where **pressure systems** are moving.

Using all this information they can **forecast** the weather up to a month in advance. They predict drought by working out how climate patterns and weather will affect the amounts of water in rivers, reservoirs, **groundwater** and the soil.

Weather in one place can affect weather thousands of kilometres away. For example, warm *El Niño currents* (the red areas in the middle of the Pacific Ocean in the picture) make some places dry and other places wet.

Can people prepare for droughts?

Some countries try to plan for the next drought before it happens. They do not want to wait and try to cope with it afterwards. Their governments do this by knowing about the water they have – how much people use and how much is stored. Governments study what effects a drought would have in different areas.

Planning for the future

In some places drought would mean **famine** for the people that live there. In that case, planning might mean storing more food. In other areas, dried-up rivers might mean that fewer tourists would visit and spend money in shops and hotels. Part of a drought plan might be encouraging new businesses to start up so that local people do not rely too heavily on money from tourism.

*In Australia, rainfall maps like this are posted on the Internet. These help farmers plan what **crops** to plant or how many **livestock** to rear at particular times of year.*

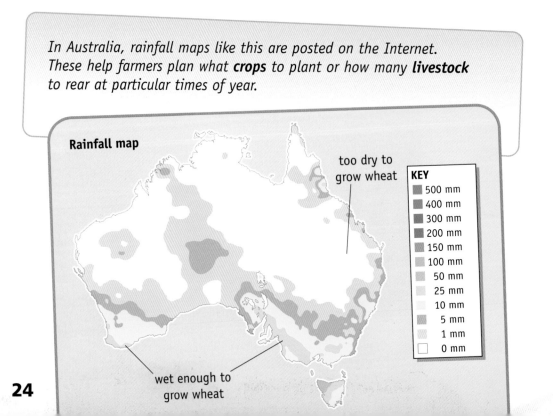

Rainfall map

too dry to grow wheat

KEY
- 500 mm
- 400 mm
- 300 mm
- 200 mm
- 150 mm
- 100 mm
- 50 mm
- 25 mm
- 10 mm
- 5 mm
- 1 mm
- 0 mm

wet enough to grow wheat

Planning for less water

The best way to plan for drought is to use less water now. This means rivers and **reservoirs** will be fuller. In our homes we can do this in many ways. We can turn off the tap when we brush our teeth, or buy a dishwasher that uses less water. City planners can plant smaller areas of lawns that need less watering and encourage people to collect and store rainwater.

Farmers can plan for drought by growing **drought-tolerant** crops. These are crops that can survive a drought, either because they need less water or have long roots that can reach underground water. They can also rear livestock that are able to thrive with less water. Some farmers can build better **irrigation** canals so crops can be watered more easily.

*In Queensland, Australia, some farmers plant salt bush plants. Salt bush can grow when it is too dry for **pasture** and provide useful **protein** for their sheep.*

Ethiopia, 1997 to 2002

Ethiopia is a poor country where people have suffered badly from many droughts. Recently they have had droughts for eight years in a row.

Now Ethiopian people – with **aid** from other countries, organizations and **charities** – are working to be better prepared when the next drought strikes. For example, they are gathering bigger stores of food and water. They are working on better drought prediction. They are also creating new health clinics so that young and elderly people will be stronger and better able to survive hard times.

DROUGHT FACTS

! Drought and **famine** have more seriously affected African countries, such as Ethiopia, than anywhere else on Earth.

! From the 1960s to 1970s, millions of people suffered and around 30 million **livestock** died.

! Many African countries were also affected by a massive drought in the 1980s to 1990s.

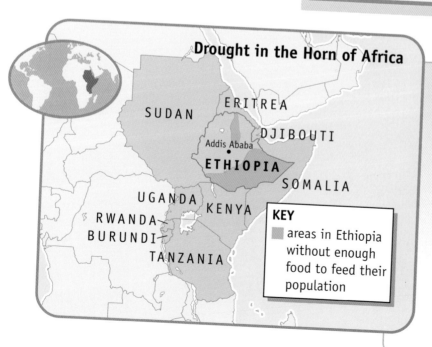

Drought in the Horn of Africa

SUDAN

ERITREA

DJIBOUTI

Addis Ababa

ETHIOPIA

SOMALIA

UGANDA

KENYA

RWANDA

BURUNDI

TANZANIA

KEY

areas in Ethiopia without enough food to feed their population

The Horn of Africa is a dry area on the edge of the Sahara desert. It is highlighted in dark green on this map. Ethiopia cannot grow enough food for its 60 million people, even when there is no drought.

Changing traditions

Traditionally, many people in the Horn of Africa were nomads. Nomads are people who move around with their animals to places with **pasture** and water, and also to get wood from trees and bushes for cooking.

In droughts there are only a few areas with healthy plants. Lots of nomads move their cattle and goats to these areas. With so much use, the plants in these places are killed and the soil is **eroded**.

The Ethiopian government and aid workers are working to encourage nomads to look after the land – for example, by teaching them to control where their animals graze. Governments help by planting **drought-tolerant crops**. They also provide the nomads with energy-efficient stoves so less wood is used in cooking and heating.

In 2002 in Ethiopia, drought planning, such as storing food aid like this, meant fewer people were affected by drought than in the past. Even so, millions of people suffered from **malnutrition**.

27

Can droughts be prevented?

Droughts are awesome forces of nature that we cannot prevent. We can help prevent the suffering that droughts bring to people's lives by predicting droughts earlier. We can also be better prepared for the problems caused by droughts.

Taking care

We also need to be careful not to make things worse. Many people believe that temperatures around the world are gradually increasing. This makes dry places even drier and more likely to have droughts. They say it is because of the greenhouse effect. When we burn fuels such as oil we release gases into the air. These gases form a layer in the air that traps heat from the sun, just as a greenhouse does. Many scientists believe that we should use fuel more carefully, to slow the warming of the Earth. Otherwise future droughts could be even worse than they are now.

We should all treat water as a precious resource instead of something we can waste.

Severe droughts of the past 100 years

1907 and 1936, China
The worst drought in history happened in the Yangtze river valley in 1907. Drought and **famine** killed an estimated 24 million people. Another 5 million died from drought and famine in 1936.

1921–22, Soviet Union
Drought in the Volga river region caused famine from 1921 to 1922. Tens of millions of people starved and as many as 5 million died.

1930–39, USA
During the 1930s fifteen US states had their lowest rainfall and highest temperatures for decades. **Crops** failed and **topsoil eroded**, causing massive dust storms that blew across the land, choking people and animals. Hundreds of thousands left their farms as **refugees**.

1965–73, Horn of Africa
For these eight years, no rain fell and 200,000 people died in north-eastern Africa. Further droughts in the 1980s and 1990s and the effects of war created millions of refugees and killed hundreds of thousands.

1965–67 and 1987–88, India
In 1965–67 drought caused crop failure and famine killed around 1.5 million people. In 1987–88 drought affected larger areas, but killed far fewer people because India was better prepared.

2000–02, USA
Much of midwestern and eastern USA had drought in 2000. The droughts caused great difficulties for farmers and increased the number of **wildfires**. These conditions continued until 2002.

Glossary

aid help that is given, such as money, medicine, food or other essential items

air pressure measurement of how strongly different bits of air push against each other

bacteria tiny living things that can cause diseases

charity group that gives out aid and makes people elsewhere aware of disasters

climate weather patterns that happen over several years

coral hard substance formed by the skeletons of tiny sea creatures over many years

crops plants grown by people for food or other uses

currents movements of water or air in particular directions

dehydration when an animal's body does not have enough water

diarrhoea illness that makes faeces (poo) very runny, causing dehydration

drought-tolerant able to grow in drought conditions

earthquake shaking of the ground caused by large movements inside the Earth

El Niño (pronounced 'el neenyo') warm water current in the Pacific Ocean that affects climate elsewhere

emergency services government-run services such as police, fire and ambulance

eroded worn away by wind, water or rubbing

famine when there is not enough food, usually for large numbers of people

firefighter man or woman who works for the fire service, fighting fires

forecast predict. A weather forecaster is someone who predicts the weather.

groundwater water found in soil or in cracks in rocks

irrigation creating canals and channels to water plants

livestock animals kept by people to eat or to sell

malnutrition illness caused by not eating enough of the right foods

pasture grass for livestock to eat

poles the north pole and the south pole – the most northerly and southerly places on Earth. They are covered in thick ice.

power plant factory making electricity

pressure system area with high or low pressure that affects the weather. In a low-pressure system air rises, creating clouds and rain; in a high-pressure system air falls, so no clouds form and the land below gets dry weather.

protein type of chemical that animals need to eat to survive. Meat and beans are two types of food containing protein.

refugee person moving to escape danger such as drought or war

reservoir large natural or specially made lake used to store water

satellite machine put into space by people to do jobs such as sending out TV signals or taking photographs

scavenger animal that finds dead animals to eat

stagnant stale water that does not move, running out of dissolved oxygen

topsoil upper layer of soil that soaks up groundwater and is ideal for growing crops

vapour gas such as steam that turns to liquid once it is cooled

volunteer person who offers help without being paid

wildfire natural fire affecting dry plants

wilt go floppy because of dryness

Find out more

Books

Eyewitness Guides: Weather, B. Cosgrove (Dorling Kindersley, 1997)

Wild Weather: Drought, Catherine Chambers (Heinemann Library, 2002)

Young Discoverers: Weather and Climate, Barbara Taylor (Kingfisher, 2002)

Websites

www.met-office.gov.uk/education – the website of the UK Met Office, with information about past weather and forecasting.

www.epa.gov/ogwdw/kids/ – the website of the US Environmental Protection Agency.

www.redcross.org/services/disaster/keepsafe/drought.html – the website of the Red Cross. Here you can find out more about ways of saving water in times of drought.

Disclaimer
All the Internet addresses (URLs) given in this book were valid at the time of going to press. However, due to the dynamic nature of the Internet, some addresses may have changed, or sites may have changed or ceased to exist since publication. While the author and publishers regret any inconvenience this may cause readers, no responsibility for any such changes can be accepted by either the author or the publishers.

Index

Titles in the *Awesome Forces of Nature* series include:

Hardback   0 431 17828 3

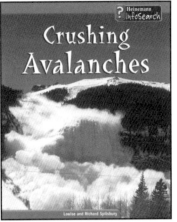

Hardback   0 431 17831 3

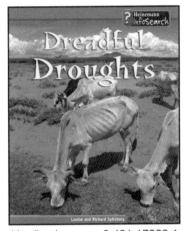

Hardback   0 431 17829 1

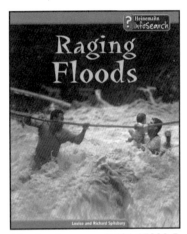

Hardback   0 431 17830 5

Hardback   0 431 17832 1

Find out about the other titles in this series on our website www.heinemann.co.uk/library